ALL GLORY

Brush Drawing Meditations on the Prayer of Consecration. by

ALLAN ROHAN CRITE

Society of Saint John the Evangelist.
Cambridge Massachusetts
1947

Printed in the United States of America
for The Society of Saint John the Evangelist
by Shea Brothers, Cambridge, Massachusetts

FOREWORD

THIS book takes its title from the first two words of the Prayer which it illustrates. The Prayer of Consecration of the American Book of Common Prayer comes down to us through the ages from that Upper Room where our Lord Jesus Christ took bread, gave thanks, brake it, and gave it to His disciples saying, "Take eat, this is my Body, which is given for you." Then He took the cup, and when He had given thanks, He gave it to them saying, "Drink ye all of this, for this is my Blood of the New Testament, which is shed for you."

Ever since that day, priests have been taking bread and wine, and saying and doing the things that Jesus Christ Himself said and did. Gradually the Prayer of Consecration took form, and crystallized. Then came additions and developments in various parts of the world. But no matter how variant the outward forms, at the heart of the Prayer the priest takes bread and wine, and says and does the things that were said and done by Christ in the Upper Room.

The Prayer of Consecration which appears in the American Book of Common Prayer has a long and interesting history. It comes to us from the persecuted Scottish Church which consecrated the first diocesan Bishop of the Anglican Church in the United States. The Scottish form of the Prayer derived through the martyred Archbishop Laud from that of the First Prayer Book of 1549, which in turn was a liberal translation of the old Latin Canon that was the Anglican Prayer of Consecration for more than nine centuries.

Mr. Crite has thoughtfully provided a "Glossary of Terms" by way of Appendix to this volume, in which are illustrated not only the vestments worn by the priest (which are only the conventionalized clothes of our Lord's time) but also some of the symbols which he has used, together with explanations.

The book has been produced as an act of homage to Christ, the Eternal Priest.

All glory be to thee, Almighty God, our heavenly Father,

for that thou, of thy tender mercy, didst give thine only Son Jesus Christ to suffer death upon the Cross for our redemption; ....

who made there (by his one oblation of himself once offered) a full, perfect, and sufficient sacrifice, oblation, and satisfaction for the sins of the whole world

and did institute, and in his holy Gospel command us
to continue, a perpetual memory of that his precious
death and sacrifice, until his coming again............

For in the night in which he was betrayed, he took Bread;
and when he had given thanks, he brake it, and gave it
to his diciples, saying, Take, eat, this is my Body, which
is given for you; Do this in remembrance of me ....

Likewise, after supper, he took the Cup: and when he had given thanks, he gave it to them, saying, Drink ye all of this; for this is my Blood of the New Testament, which is shed for you and for many, for the remission of sins; Do this, as oft as ye shall drink it in remembrance of me.

Wherefore, O Lord and heavenly Father, according to the institution of thy dearly beloved Son our Saviour Jesus Christ, we, thy humble servants, do celebrate and make here before thy Divine Majesty, with these thy holy gifts, which we now offer unto thee, the memorial thy Son hath commanded us to make; having in remembrance his blessed passion —

and precious death

his mighty resurrection

and glorious ascension; rendering unto thee most hearty thanks for the innumerable benefits procured unto us by the same.

And we most humbly beseech thee, O merciful Father, to hear us; and of thy almighty goodness, vouchsafe to bless and sanctify with thy Word and Holy Spirit, ...

these thy gifts and creatures of bread and wine;

that we receiving them according to thy Son our
Saviour Jesus Christ's holy institution in remembrance
of his death and passion,

may be partakers of his most blessed Body and Blood.

And we earnestly desire thy fatherly goodness, mercifully to accept this our sacrifice of praise and thanksgiving; most humbly beseeching thee to grant that,

by the merits and death of thy Son Jesus Christ, and through faith in his blood, we, and all thy whole Church, may obtain remission of our sins, and all other benefits of his passion

And here we offer and present unto thee, O Lord, our selves, our souls and bodies, to be a reasonable, holy, and living sacrifice unto thee; humbly beseeching thee,

that we, and all others who shall be partakers of this Holy Communion, may worthily receive the most precious Body and Blood of thy Son Jesus Christ, be filled with thy grace and heavenly benediction and made one body with him, that he may dwell in us, and we in him. And although we are unworthy, through our manifold sins, to offer unto thee any sacrifice; yet we beseech thee to accept this our bounden duty and service; not weighing our merits, but pardoning our offences,

through Jesus Christ our Lord; by whom, and with whom, in the unity of the Holy Ghost, all honour and glory be unto thee, O Father Almighty, world without end.

Amen

Glossary of Terms

Glossary of Terms

vestments

amice

cassock

amice

alb

cincture

stole

maniple

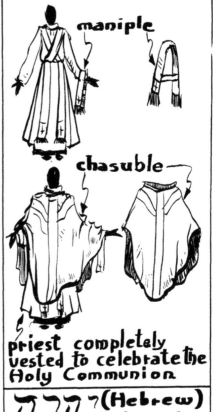

chasuble

priest completely
vested to celebrate the
Holy Communion

יהוה (Hebrew)
Jehovah

A Ω (Greek)
Alpha and Omega
beginning and end
A title of Jesus and
Rev. chapt. 1 ⌐GOD.
verse. 11

two candles
signify the
two natures
of Christ
Divine and
human

Terms

ihs (abbreviation for Iŋsous (greek) Jesus

Hand of God.

Seraphim or Cherubim may be represented as having 6, 4, or 2 wings

Dove is Holy Spirit

7 flames 7 gifts of the Holy

Spirit — Wisdom
Understanding
Counsel
Fortitude
Knowledge
Piety
Holy Fear

dalmatic

This is based on the very ancient way of depicting the Crucifixion showing Christ in a **dalmatic**

This type halo used only on the Persons of the Holy Trinity
God The Father
God The Son
God The Holy Spirit

Christ shown as head of Church completely rested as bishop having complete authority

— maniple
— pallium (worn only by archbishops Metropolitans, patriarchs and popes)
— chasuble
— dalmatic
— alb
— stole
— There is a tunicle similar to dalmatic in shape but shorter.

INRI initials for
Iesus
Nazarenus
Rex
Iudaeorū
Latin for Jesus of Nazareth King of the Jews.

Terms

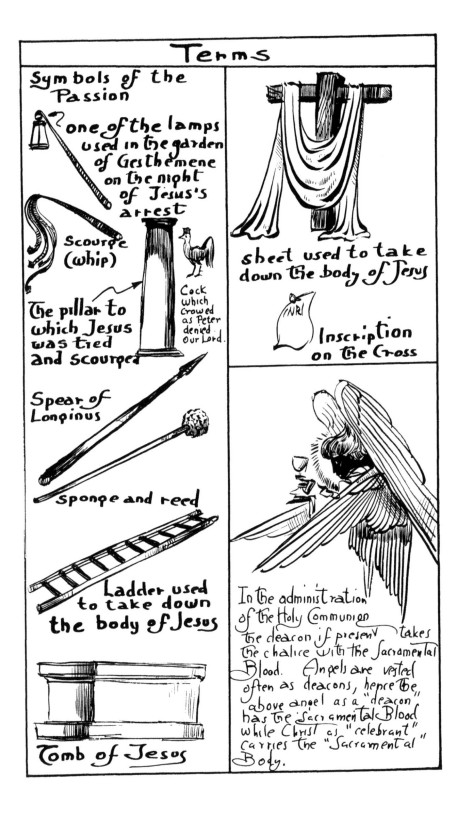

Symbols of the Passion

one of the lamps used in the garden of Gethsemene on the night of Jesus's arrest

Scourge (whip)

Cock which crowed as Peter denied our Lord.

The pillar to which Jesus was tied and scourged

Spear of Longinus

sponge and reed

Ladder used to take down the body of Jesus

Tomb of Jesus

sheet used to take down the body of Jesus

INRI

Inscription on the Cross

In the administration of the Holy Communion the deacon if present takes the chalice with the sacramental Blood. Angels are vested often as deacons, hence the above angel as a "deacon" has the sacramental Blood while Christ as "celebrant" carries the "Sacramental" Body.